# THIS JOURNAL BELONGS TO

Ⓒ 2020 BLACK HISTORY AMONG US PUBLISHING

INSIDE THIS JOURNAL THERE ARE 29 FUN AND ENGAGING PROMPTS FOR EACH DAY OF FEBRUARY THAT CAN BE USED BY PARENTS OR TEACHERS TO EDUCATE STUDENTS ABOUT WOMEN IN BLACK HISTORY.

ANSWER THE PROMPTS ABOUT EACH HISTORICAL FIGURE.

ALSO ADD SOME FUN FACTS ABOUT YOURSELF!

HAPPY WRITING!

What were some of Coretta Scott King's accomplishments? Name two other female leaders from the civil rights movement?

What is Ruth E. Carter known for? What is your favorite superhero movie?

Who was Mahalia Jackson and how did she have an impact on the "I Have A Dream" speech? What is your favorite song?

How did Venus and Serena Williams have an impact on tennis? Have you ever played tennis?

# Why is Harriet Tubman's story significant? What are two questions that you would ask her?

How did Ida B. Wells have an impact on the civil rights movement? Name two other civil rights leaders (male or female).

How did Hattie McDaniel have an impact on Hollywood?
What was the last movie that you saw?

What was Dr. Mary McLeod Bethune's biggest accomplishments? What's your favorite subject?

What was Lena Horne famous for? What are some of your favorite movies?

What is the importance of Ruby Bridges life on education in America? What subjects do you like the most?

What was Claudette Colvin's contribution to the civil rights movement? Have you ever taken a bus trip?

# Phillis Wheatley is a historical figure because.... Do you have a favorite poet?

# Who were two of NASA's human computers? What is your favorite computer game?

What did Dr. Mae Jemison do that was out of this world? What are some extraordinary things that you have done?

# What did Mary Jane Patterson do? What college would you like to attend?

Why was Shirley Chisholm so influential? If you were President what would you change?

What were some of Constance Baker Motley's biggest accomplishments and what are some of your biggest accomplishments?

Maya Angelou's story is significant to black history because… What are two of your favorite poems?

# What obstacles did Wilma Rudolph overcome and how do they inspire you?

Who was the first African American First Lady? If you could ask her anything what would you ask?

How did Misty Copeland change ballet? Who are a few of your favorite dancers?

What sport did Althea Gibson have an impact on? What are some of your favorite sports?

Who was Zora Neale Hurston? What are some of your favorite books?

How did Madame C.J. Walker revolutionize the beauty industry? Who does your hair?

What were a few of Bessie Coleman's accomplishments? Do you like to fly?

What did Fannie Lou Hamer fight for? What are some things that you are not afraid to stand up for?

What did Sojourner Truth do? Name two other abolitionists.

How did Henrietta Lacks change medicine? Name two African American doctors.

Who was Angela Davis? Name two of Angela Davis' quotes.

Printed in the USA
CPSIA information can be obtained
at www.ICGtesting.com
LVHW082233170124
769269LV00042B/2060